VIEWS OF
1888 BERKSWELL 1988

B. Marshall.

ALBERT SMITH

**SIMANDA PRESS,
BERKSWELL, 1988.**

The compiler would welcome comments and further information. These may be addressed to Simanda Press, Berkswell, 1 Meriden Road, Berkswell, Coventry. CV7 7BE.

Printed by Warwick Printing Co. Ltd., Theatre Street, Warwick
© Albert Smith
ISBN 0 9513867 0 0

CONTENTS

INTRODUCTION

On Friday 3rd. August 1888, fate was to dictate that the village of Berkswell was to remain the unique village that it is today, for, on that day, the estate of the late Mr. Thomas Walker was put up for sale at the King's Head Hotel, Coventry.

Of the 39 lots on offer, lots one and two formed the largest part of the original estate. Lot one comprised Berkswell Hall with the well timbered park and twelve dairy farms, numerous cottages and small dwellings, in all containing 1530 acres, 2 roods and 18 perches. Lot two was the estate known as Mercote Hall and comprised the residence with stables, farm homesteads, Park Farm, Mercote Mill, together with several cottages, in all, 410 acres, 3 roods and 12 perches.

Had these two lots been sold separately, much of the character of the village would have been lost over the years as, undoubtedly, the estate would have been broken up, the fine timber in the park sold for profit and the land used for other purposes.

However, luckily for Berkswell, the bidding for each lot did not reach the reserve and the two lots were sold privately afterwards, an offer being accepted from an agent acting for Mr. Joshua Hirst Wheatley of Mirfield, Yorkshire.

Over the years that followed, much good work was undertaken, additional cottages being erected for estate workers and, in 1900 the Reading Room was donated to the village to improve the social life.

After the death of Mr. Wheatley in 1925, his son Colonel Charles Joshua Hirst Wheatley and his wife moved to the Hall from Hill House and continued to manage the estate in a caring manner until his own sudden death in 1943 at the early age of 55. This could have brought disastrous consequences for Berkswell except for the fortitude of his widow, Christobel, who continued to run the estate as before for a further 40 years and did much in that time to protect the village from change, due to her strength of character as a member of Meriden Rural Distrct Council and Berkswell Parish Council. Unfortunately Mrs. Wheatley died at the age of 89 on the 31st. December 1987, only hours before the year commenced that would commemorate her family's 100 years association with Berkswell, and the compiler of this book would like to dedicate it to this remarkable lady and also to all parishioners, past and present, who have, through their hard work, contributed towards making Berkswell what it is today.

In addition to publishing this book to celebrate this centenary, as it will be issued at a time when the possible fate of the village is being decided at a public enquiry, it is hoped that those who glance through these pages will give thought to the sacrifices that have been made in the past and will not give up lightly the unique heritage that has been left to us.

The compiler would like to thank the many kind friends who permitted their postcards and photographs to be reproduced in this book and also those who gave moral support at times when publication seemed impossible.

Albert Smith
Berkswell 1988

"Reproduced from the 1887 Ordnance Survey Map"

THE VILLAGE

An aerial view taken in the late 1930's and used as a Christmas Card by Mrs. Wheatley, this one being sent to Mrs. Dolly Webber. The view shows the centre of the village, with Berkswell Hall in the background and the Rectory still it's original size with the gardens extending right through to Lavender Hall Lane.

The Church of St. John Baptist, as it looked in 1888. This fine Norman Church, built about 1150, is thought to have been built around an earlier Saxon Church possibly built by a Saxon land owner as a mark of thanks following Baptism in the nearby Well, around which the original settlement would have evolved.

Interior of Berkswell Church

c 1936. (Thompson, Coventry). This interior view of Berkswell Church shows the numerous pendant and standard paraffin lamps which had to be attended to by the Verger. The White stone Pulpit was removed to be built into a Church at Tile Hill, but this was never built and the fate of the Pulpit remains a mystery.

The attraction of Berkswell is nothing new, these Edwardian ladies have obviously cycled to the village and are shown sitting on the grass outside the porch with their cameras ready to record the visit.

c 1905. The lane leading from Old Lane, now Lavender Hall Lane to the Well. The cottage known as 'Spring Villa' can be seen on the right. This cottage which was eventually demolished to make way for the garages which now stand on this site, was the headquarters of the Berkswell Scouts before they moved to the new premises.

c 1912. (C.W. Selby, Saltley, Birm). This postcard shows the attraction running water will always have to children. Gathered around the Well are Horace Radford on the left, Alex Lower centre, Ida Barnett unfortunately due to die shortly afterwards and on the right a friend from Bradnocks Marsh.

This picture taken in the mid 1920's shows very clearly the near poverty which existed following the 1914/18 War. Except for Nellie Kaye holding the baby, Lucy Callow standing behind the pram, and Charlie Woolley with the cap, most of the other children are 'Peakes', a large family who lived in the small cottage leading to the Well, known as 'Spring Villa'.

Teddy Barr's wife seen here fetching her daily water from the Well. This was a common sight in the village as prior to piped water arriving in 1940, every home used Well water or water from the various pumps, at the crossroads or in certain gardens. The use of this water possibly contributing to the longevity of the villagers.

The Rectory, Berkswell.

c 1936 (Thompson, Cov). The Rectory, now the Well House, shown here as it would have looked in 1888, when the Rector was Rev. Henry William Watson. Fame had already come to Berkswell at that time as the Rector's two daughters Maud (19) and Lilian (26) met each other at Wimbledon in the 1884 Womans Tennis Championship, which Maud won to become the first Ladies Wimbledon Champion. She was awarded the MBE for Nursing Service in the 1914/18 War.

A view of the Rectory, now the Well house, when used during the 1914/18 War as a hospital for wounded soldiers, the Commandant Miss M.E.E. (Maud) Watson being shown seated in the middle of the group with the Rector's wife, Mrs. Back shown standing to the right. *(W. Holmes, Birm).*

c 1909 (Leafy Leam, L.Spa) This postcard is believed to show William Dingle, who was a farmer at Bradnock's Marsh in the 1880's and by the time this card was produced was a resident in the Almshouses.

THE "STOCKS" BERKSWELL

This postcard issued in the early 1920's shows a view looking down Old Lane, now Lavender Hall Lane, with the stocks and Almshouses to the right and the old cottages which were replaced by the estate bungalows, on the left.

The Meet shown assembling on the top of the Village Green, before moving through the Black Gate to the left of the picture past where the scout hut now is, on to the Park. This picture must have been taken during the first War as some of the wounded soldiers who were at that time patients at the Rectory Hospital can be seen to the left of the picture.

This postcard, issued in the early 1930's, taken on the Green from behind the stocks, looking towards the Bear crossroads shows the original elms before they were replaced. The enamel signs on the wall and gates of the shop include 'Will's Wild Woodbines' and 'Colman's Starch'.

c. 1908 (Frederick Lewis, Birm). This view of Church Lane shows a delightful group of children outside their cottages posing for the photographer. A trap is at the gates of the church.

A view of Church Lane in the early 1920's with the Photographer's Motor Cycle and Sidecar outside Mrs. Bausers door. This cottage from which sweets were sold to the school children has a notice stating 'Mineral Waters' over the door.

This tranquil scene, taken at the point where Berkswell Lane from Balsall Common met Old Lane in the village, now Lavender Hall Lane, shows a family group captured about 1906 entering the village with Beehive Cottage directly in front.

c. 1905. Mrs. Owen seen standing at the door of Beehive Cottage. Her husband Mr. William Owen was responsible for keeping the Key of the animal Pound on the Coventry Road.

c 1906. (Frederic Lewis, Birm). This group of cottages thought to be an old Coaching Inn, were next to Beehive cottage which can be seen just beyond the end of the building. These were demolished to enable the estate to build new retired workers bungalows in the 1950's.

This postcard issued in 1908, shows a group of village children on the godcake at the rear of the Almshouses. These were built in 1853 from charity funds to accommodate 12 aged persons from the Parish. The view also shows the small cottage before the gables were added in the roof, which now houses the museum.

A LIST OF BERKSWELL CHARITIES
compiled from Ancient Records

Name of Charity	Date of Foundation	Nature of Original Gift
Berkswell Church School & Poor Lands Charity	This is the oldest of the Charities and was said to have existed "from time immemorial" in a late 16th Century Court Action.	
Good Friday Grove Charity	1519 By will of Rowland Robinson	Rent from three pieces of land called Good Friday Grove.
Freckleton's Gift	1592 By will of Leonard Freckleton	6/8 a year from a field near Springfield Hall, Knowle.
Marsh's Gift	1618	10/- a year to be paid from a field at Barston.
Miles' Gift		10/- a year from Stone Pit Fields to be distributed amongst the poor on St. Thomas' Day.
Potter Gift	By will of Job Potter	£1-10-0 a year to be paid out of the Kendall Field to be distributed amongst the poor in bread upon St. Thomas' Day.
Thomas Docker's Gift		5/- a year from Hither Waste Field to be distributed amongst the poor in bread on St. Thomas' Day.
Gilbert Docker's Gift	1730	5/- a year from a house and land in Docker's Lane.
Whitehead Gift	1701 By will of John Whitehead	Land in Oldhall End the income from which is to be used for setting forth young persons as apprentices and to be distributed amongst the poor.
Catherine Whitehead's Gift	1711 By will of Catherine Whitehead	30/- a year to be distributed with the John Whitehead Gift.
Sleath's Gift	1729 By will of William Sleath	10/- a year to be paid out of the Coppice Wood called Round Readings and to be distributed amongst the Poor in Bread.
Cattell's Charity	1833 By will of Rev. Thomas Cattell	Interest on certain securities to be used for the repair of the Gallery in Church.
Huddesford Charity	1836 By codicil to the will of Elizabeth Huddesford	£5-13-8 to be distributed each year amongst the poor.
Reynolds Charity	1905 By will of Reynolds	£1-17-10 to be distributed each year amongst the poor.

Although the Charity Gifts shown here seem small by todays standards, in 1925 Mr. Hitchcock's could provide quite a treat for eleven villagers from the £1—17—10 Reynolds Charity.

This picture of Grocer and Provision Dealer Mr. W. Hitchcock's Shop, taken in the late 1920's, looks little different to the Village Stores as it is today. Mr. Hitchcocks who was also the verger of the church, had the responsibility of lighting, trimming and extinguishing the paraffin lamps in the church, before electricity came in 1938.

A group of china crested figures from the authors collection. These souvenir items were very popular in the 1930's, and the demand from visitors to the village obviously resulted in the Shopkeeper ordering a supply, the underside of the figures stating "Made for Hitchcocks, The Stores, Berkswell."

A. CARTER & SONS

VILLAGE STORES

BEST QUALITY
GROCERIES & PROVISIONS
also
FRUIT :: **BOOT REPAIRS**

Alfie Carter who worked for Berkswell Estate took over the Village Store in the mid 1930's but did not make a success of running the business, one reason being his son's over-generous nature with his school friends with the sweet stock.

c 1936 (Thompson, Cov). A postcard showing Bear Crossroads, looking up Coventry Road. The house shown to the right is Meadow Bank, which was built by Mr. Charles Hope for his own occupation in the early part of this century when he was a builder working from premises directly behind the building on the left.

A view of the first pair of estate cottages on Meriden Road, at the Bear crossroads. The Policeman is thought to be P.C. Bobby White who at the time of this postcard in the early 1920's lived at the second of these cottages. *(W. Holmes, Birm).*

c. 1905. (Frederic Lewis, Birm). The second pair of estate cottages on Meriden Road, like the first pair were the only cottages, with the exception of the thatched cottage, to exist on this road in 1888. The cottage nearest the camera was the village Post Office, the notice over the doorway also indicating that Amos Webb, Tailor was the postmaster at this time.

The view on this postcard is looking towards Meriden, showing the Post Office on the right, the large noticeboard being outside the policeman's house. The card would be issued during the 1914-18 War as two soldiers are to be seen sitting on the bank. The railings shown outside the houses were removed to aid the War effort during the Second World War. The girl on the bicycle is Barbara Howe.

This postcard posted in 1910 shows a typical rural scene of that period with a group of children on the way home from school and two farm carts travelling up Station Road, now Spencers Lane. The man sitting in the gateway would be a milestone inspector (Tramp).

c 1906. (Frederic Lewis, Birm). The thatched cottage on the Meriden Road, with the roof of Mr. Charles Hope's Builders Yard seen on the right. The name of the girl in the garden is not known, but in later years Mrs Hazeldine, the sister of Mr. Hope, lived here and is remembered as a very kind lady.

The Reading Room, Berkswell.

c 1912. The Reading Room, Meriden Road, which by this time was being used for numerous functions including a Billiards Club. The members shown in the register include Rev Hugh Back, the Rector at that time. The lady seen at the gates of the next cottage is thought to be Mrs. Gibbs with her sons Jim and Harold.

READING ROOM. BERKSWELL

c 1915. (Sidwell, Meriden.) The Reading Room, Meriden Road, the foundation stone layed by Edith Adele, wife of Joshua Hirst Wheatley on 12th November 1900. The Reading Room built and given to the village by Mr. Wheatley, to provide a place to hold social events, had the internal fittings provided by Miss Lant, another local benefactor from Nailcote Hall.

This postcard, posted in 1910, shows the Bear Inn with a group of lads standing by the village pump, which, like the signpost, seems to be covered with notices including one advertising grazing land for rent. The Crimean gun seen outside the front of the Bear, on Queen Victoria's Diamond Jubilee, was apparently taken to the top of Bear Hill, filled with black powder, and fired, which shattered most of the windows in the village.

c. 1937 (Thompson Cov.). The Bear Inn at the time when the publican, as shown by the sign over the door, was Alfred Winter. It is thought that the bicycle against the wall with a double crossbar belonged to Archie Cudmore, the gamekeeper at Berkswell Hall. The notice by the village pump is advertising a fete at Tile Hill.

c. 1905 (Frederick Lewis, Birm.). This postcard shows the Bear Inn with the Meriden Road in the distance. This 16th century Inn which was part of the Berkswell Estate and was the venue for the annual Stattis (Hiring) Fair, was sold by the Estate in 1951.

THE FOLLOWING
REWARDS
WILL BE PAID ON CONVICTION OF THE OFFENDERS FOR THE
UNDERMENTIONED OFFENCES
BY THE MEMBERS OF THE
BERKSWELL ASSOCIATION
FOR THE

PROTECTION OF LIFE & PROPERTY & THE PROSECUTION OF FELONS

MURDER	20 0 0
Burglary	10 0 0
Highway or Footpad Robbery	10 0 0
Setting Fire to any Buildings, Ricks, Stacks, or other Effects	10 0 0
Stealing or Maiming any Horse, Mare, Gelding, Cow, Calf, Sheep, Lambs, or Pigs	10 0 0
Breaking into (in the night) any Hen-house or other Buildings, and Stealing Poultry thereout	5 0 0
Breaking into, and Stealing Corn or other Grain (threshed), out of Barn or other Buildings, or receiving the same knowing it to be stolen	5 0 0
Receiving Stolen Goods, knowing them to be stolen	3 0 0
Stealing Poultry in daytime, or Killing, Maiming, or otherwise destroying any other Animal belonging to a Member of this Association	2 0 0
Stealing any Corn or other Grain (unthreshed) any straw or fodder	2 0 0
Stealing Implements of Husbandry, or Ironwork belonging thereto	1 0 0
Cutting, or carrying away, any Timber, or other Trees, or any Wood or Underwood, or Breaking or Stealing any Locks, Gates, Stiles, Boards, Planks, Posts, Rails, Faggots, or Coals	1 0 0
Stealing Fish by Nets or otherwise (in the night)	1 0 0
Stealing any Peas, Beans, Turnips, Carrots, Potatoes, or other Roots, Fruits, or Vegetables, out of any Field, Garden, or Orchard, or Breaking or Stealing any Fence, Hedge, or other Mounds, belonging thereto	0 10 0
For Stealing or taking Fish (in the daytime)	0 10 0

And for any other Felonious Act, not before particularly mentioned, such Rewards as the Committee shall think proper to allow; and they will also reward any Policeman, Constable, or any other person, by whose information any person shall be apprehended to conviction, who has injured any Member of this Society in person or property, for the discovery of which the above Rewards are offered.

Any accomplice making a discovery shall be entitled to the same Rewards, and every means used to obtain a pardon

MR. R. MILBOURNE. ⎱
MR. C. HOPE.   ⎰ Trustees.
MR. C. HITCHCOCKS. ⎰

SUBSCRIBERS.

All Accounts against the Association to be sent to the Secretary on or before the 1st day of June. 1905

CURRIDGE, "STANDARD" OFFICE, COVENTRY.

THE BEAR INN,
Proprietor: A. WINTER.

PHONE: BERKSWELL 2.
HIGH-CLASS CATERING.
FREE HOUSE.

BERKSWELL
NEAR COVENTRY.

June 13, 1928

Berkswell Association
Prosecution of Felons

40 Dinners @ 5/6		11	0	0
Beer Served with Dinner		1	1	4
33 Scotch Whiskeys @ 8ᵈ { Drinks with Association }		1	2	0
Beer Ex.ᵃ			5	0
Room for Meeting			5	0
	£	13	13	4

Rec'd With Thanks
June 14/28
A. Winter

Berkswell Association for the Prosecution of Felons, formed prior to 1790, issued this poster in 1905 and shows rewards offered after successful prosecution in respect to varying offences. Although no murderers have been apprehended in recent years, a dinner is held annually and in 1928 Alfred Winter at the Bear Inn provided a meal for 40 members for a total, including room charge and drinks, of £13-13s-4d as seen on this receipt.

This postcard posted in 1915 shows the crossroads with the Bear Inn on the left and the entrance of the Cafe Gardens on the right. The uneven surface of the road does not appear to deter the two cyclists seen on their way up what is now Spencers Lane, towards Carol Green.

A view of the inside of the Garden Cafe when first opened by Cornelius Charles Lilly in 1910. The cafe which became a popular meeting place for both visitors and villagers was acquired by Mr and Mrs Hadley in 1938, following the death of Mr. Lilly. The property which was part of the Berkswell Estate was finally sold in the 1960's and has now been divided into two, The Malt House and The Garden House.

The rear view of the Garden Cafe in the late 1930's, with the "Bear Inn" shown in the background. At that time Mrs. Hadley's home was the portion of the building on the left which is now The Garden House.

An account settled by Mrs. Dawson in 1931 for work carried out by Mr. Charles Woolley.

GARDEN CAFE BERKSWELL

1½ miles from Berkswell Station L.M.S., opposite the Bear Inn.

SAMUEL DAVY & SON

Instructed by the Representative of the late Mr. C. C. Lilly, Will Sell by Auction, on

SATURDAY, MARCH 5, 1938
AT 2 P.M. PUNCTUALLY, the Useful Household

FURNITURE

CATERING EFFECTS

Including Brass and Iron Bedsteads, Iron Stove, Chairs, Pictures, Invalid Bed-Table, Washstands, CHESTS OF DRAWERS, Mirrors, Toilet Ware, Painted Wardrobe,

2 ANTIQUE OAK CORNER CUPBOARDS
Kitchen Tables, SUITE comprising 6 Chairs and Couch, Overmantels, Bookcases, Kitchen Utensils, Kitchen Dressers,

60 BENTWOOD CHAIRS
12 DEAL TABLES, 3ft. 9in. x 2ft.

Trestle Tables, 3 Copper Urns, Table-Tennis Table, Plate Racks, Meat Safes, Hanging Lamps, Matting, Large Quantity Crockery, 2 Meat Jacks,

30 GARDEN CHAIRS AND TABLES
9 Deck Chairs, Six 6ft. Garden Seats, Tennis Marker, Carpenter's Bench, Fowl Houses, &c. &c.

NO CATALOGUES.

Auctioneers' Offices : Knowle, nr. Birmingham, and 23, Hertford Street, Coventry.

A sale notice of the Garden Cafe Contents when sold in 1938.

The Berkswell Forge as it looked in 1923, Charles Woolley Junior is seen in the group on the right holding his younger brother Ken, Anne his sister is to the left and his other brother Jack and sister Margery are on the right. Charlie Golds horse is awaiting his new shoes. The beautiful iron railings were cut off for scrap in the second war.

c 1934. (Walker). This view looking down Station Road, now Spencers Lane, shows a horse and cart outside the Forge, with The Priory on the left and Village Farm just showing behind.

This view taken outside Village Farm in the 1880's shows the dress of the children and the type of perambulator that was used to take their younger brother down to the shop.

c. 1906 (Frederic Lewis, Birm.). The view on this postcard is taken from the back of the Priory at a time when Alfred Smith, the gardener at The Moat and his wife were in occupation.

BERKSWELL HALL

The Lodge to Berkswell Hall on the Meriden Road shown on this 1920 postcard with the original large acorns on the gateposts. The acorn on right has since disintegrated, a new one, turned by Jack Woolley on his wood lathe at the Forge, has recently been fitted.

The clock tower which stood on top of the stable block. Although this was eventually demolished this picture was taken some years before, when the tower was being repaired. The hands on the face shown and on the opposite face were removed as it was found that the mechanism was not powerful enough to drive all sets of hands and only the dials facing the Hall and the driveway had hands.

c 1905. (Frederic Lewis, Birm). The Main Entrance Hall showing the imposing Iron Railings and Gates, with the carriageways leading to the left to the Entrance Lodge on the Birmingham Road, and to the right to the Lodge on the Meriden Road.

c 1905. (Frederic Lewis. Birm). A view of Berkswell Hall from the side showing the orangery. The Hall was rebuilt in 1812 and enlarged to give five Reception Rooms, Nineteen Principal Bed and Dressing Rooms, and Eleven Servants' Bedrooms, by the time the hall was sold in 1888.

Colonel Charles Joshua Hirst Wheatley at his desk dealing with everyday problems at Berkswell Hall in the 1930's.

A view taken in the old drawing room at Berkswell Hall sometime in the 1930's. This room was eventually divided at a point where the column is situated, the door behind the column then leading into a new dining room. The two fireplaces are still retained in two of the flats into which Berkswell Hall has now been converted.

30

The Meet having a rest at Berkswell Hall, a small table with drinks at the ready are on the lawn the other side of the Ha-Ha wall. The Orangery can also be seen and also one of the large Wellingtonia conifers.

Bert Wagstaff the Chauffeur at Berkswell Hall seen beside a Rolls-Royce in the stable yard. He stated that of the six cars at the Hall, he much preferred to drive the Armstrong Siddeley when taking 'Miss Ann' back to school at Cambridge, as the long bonnet and large headlamps on the Rolls made it almost impossible to see the road ahead in the fog.

Staff at the Hall in the early 1920's. From the left Bert Wagstaff (Chauffeur), Miss. A. Thompson, who became Mrs Ernie Webb (Housemaid), Mrs. Senior (Cook) and Jack Mills (Groom).

c 1910. (M. Watson, Berk.). This postcard which shows Berkswell Hall from across the Park Pool, was sent by Mary at Blind Hall, to a friend in Coventry.

c 1906 (Frederic Lewis, Birm). Children shown on the park footbridge with the Carriage Drive bridge which took carriages from Berkswell Hall to the Top Lodge on the Brimingham Road, behind them.

c 1906. (Frederic Lewis, Birm.). The Top Lodge, Birmingham Road, shown with it's original thatched roof.

SCHOOL LIFE

Outside the school in 1888. Although the picture is of poor quality it is well worth including to show the dress of the girls at the time, also this is the only known picture of John William Nicholl, the Headmaster.

Group I at Berkswell Church of England School in 1908 shows Miss Pollard who was in charge of the Infants. Although the names of the back row are not known, the middle row from the left are Misses Sibley and Lower, Chris Rone, Rose Timms, * , Bert Mundy, Jim Webb, Gill Fletcher and Cath Owen. Front row, * , Clara Owen, Miss Hillard, Sid Underhill, Millicent Kaye, Doris Higgs, Hannah Mundy.

Group 2 also shows Miss Pollard so this must be the remainder of the infants class. The names of very few of the children are known but Ida Barnett who is on the extreme right front row, was to die a few years later at the age of only nine, an indication of the hard life of the children some of which had to walk from as far away as Bradnocks Marsh to the school.

Group 3 shows Mrs Frewing who was the Headmaster's Wife and was in charge of Standards 3 and 4. Again the names of very few of the children are known, but Len Skidmore has named the girls second from the left in the two middle rows as his sisters Adah and Lucy. A picture of the Headmaster, Mr. Frewing's Group has never been seen by the author, he being in charge of Standards 5, 6 and 7.

Although the same board is being used and indicates No. 5 the date is not shown but is also thought to be 1908. The teacher is believed to be Miss Thornton who was in charge of Standards 1 and 2 at that time.

c 1910. A classrooom scene at Miss Downes Grove School, which was in the Gardens of Grove Cottage, on the spot now occupied by the Scout Hut. Miss Downes who is seen on the right opened this special school in 1904 after teaching for a short time at the Church School. Her ability was such that many of her students acheived successes in numerous subjects.

Girls from Berkswell School practicing their Maypole Dance sometime in the early 1920's. The maypole is shown behind the Church in what is now the Cremation ground, the wall of the Rectory is shown on the right.

The Grove School ... Berkswell ...

MISTRESS:

Miss H. L. DOWNES, Inter. B.A. Lond.

First Class Matriculation, First Class College of Preceptors.
Student of Mason University College, and of Birmingham
———— University ————

Who holds Testimonials from the following Professors and Teachers:

Rev. H. W. WATSON, Sc.D., M.A., F.R.S.
Rector of Berkswell

Prof. R. S. HEATH. D.Sc., M.A.
Vice-Principal and Professor of Mathematics in the University of Birmingham.

Prof. E. A. SONNENSCHEIN, D.Litt., Oxon.
Dean of the Faculty of Arts and Professor of Latin and Greek in the University of Birmingham.

Prof. W. MACNEILE DIXON, Litt.D., LL.B.
Professor of English in the University of Birmingham.

Prof. H. G. FIELDER, M.A., Ph.D.
Professor of German and Germanic Philology in the University of Birmingham.

TERMS :

School Fees - - - -	~~Three~~ 4 Guineas per Terms	
Boys over Nine - - -	Four Guineas ,, ,,	
Music - - - -	One and Half Guineas ,, ,,	

Private lessons in French, Classics, and Higher Mathematics.
Terms on application.

Successes gained by Pupils include :

London Matriculation,	Cambridge Locals.
L.R.A.M.	A.L.C.M.

Associated Board and Trinity College Local Examinations in Music
Scholarships and Entrance Examinations into High Schools

ONE TERM'S NOTICE REQUIRED BEFORE LEAVING.
ALL FEES PAYABLE IN ADVANCE.

A leaflet of approx 1920 giving details of the Grove School. The Terms seem high for that time but could be justified by the successes which were achieved.

A Certificate Awarded by Her Majesty's Inspector in 1889 to Arthur Scarsbrook at the Church of England School. The Rector Henry William Watson signing the award.

Berkswell School Group with Headmaster Mr. Joseph F. Frewing in 1928. The children are back row from left: Harold Gibbs, Eric Howes, George Osborne, John Pettifor, Frank Bull, Bill Freeman and Harry Bicknell. Front row: Margery Woolley, Doris Pointon, Peggy Frewing (Headmaster's daughter), Grace Willoughby, Doris Houghton, Doris Newcombe, Bessie Parker, Dorothy Long and Doris Pinks.

This 1928 School Picture is thought to be Mrs Frewing's Class, she possibly being indisposed at the time. The children are from left back row: Harold Waterson, Geof Pointon, Bert Waterson, Ron Cooper, Arthur Pettifor, Tom Bassett, Bill Dyer, Albert Tidmarsh, Ron Webb and Bill Hurst. Middle row: Violet Houghton, Marjorie Newcombe, Molly Leeson, Gladys Houghton, Nora Evans, Doris Bartholomew, Irene Glover, Alice Ayres, Phyllis Pettifor and Patricia Leeson. Front row: Leanord (Welshie) Thomas, Roland Carter, John Woolley, Brynis Jones, Mary Dickinson, Francis Glover, Walter Pinks, Fred Pinks and Roland Fletcher.

Another 1928 group, this time the infants with their very well loved teacher Miss Margaret Shaddock, who travelled everyday from Kenilworth by train. The children back row from left, Freddie Pope, John Whitehead, Bill Evans, Bill Pettifor, Tom Bartholomew, Peter Sheepy, Leonard Dickinson, Frank Bicknell, Sid Ford, and Ken Woolley. Middle Row. Sylvia Chattaway, Grace Sweatman, Mary Wilkes, Kathleen Osborne, Ivy Osborne, Doreen Webb, Janet Woolley and Mary Tidmarsh. Front row. Betty Thomas, Daisy Evans, Annie Phillimore, Maud Carter, Phyllis Pointon and Nancy Hurford.

Mrs. Callow passing the time of day with a neighbour, sometime in the mid 1930's, the girls with the bicycles being from Miss Downes' Grove special school, having just emerged from the path to Grove Cottage.

This picture postcard issued in 1932 shows groups of School children possibly taken at lunchtime, the three children on the right being Ken Woolley, brother Jack and their friend Charlie Fox with the bicycle. The group under the trees on the village green include Eric Pinks, Sid Ford and George Hawksford.

A view of the schoolchildren in front of the Church gates in 1953. The Headmistress, Miss Gwendolene Tattersall who came to the school in 1936, is shown in the centre of the group, Mrs James is to the right and Miss Mulligan, who became Mrs Innis Brett on the left.

EARNING A LIVING

Charles Woolley Senior as a young man at his original premises in Benton Green Lane, which stood on the spot where 'Temple Cloud' now stands. His father, also Charles, is on the left, and his brother John on the right.

Charles Woolley Senior inside the Berkswell Forge demonstrating an early hand drill. He moved to the Forge from Benton Green Lane in 1910.

This picture taken at Hawker's Moor Farm in the early 1930's shows Ada Abbott, wife of William Abbott who was the tenant farmer, on the right, and her sister Rebecca Brown on the left. Seated on the left, Tom Thompson and his wife with a young Bob on her lap, and Bill, Mrs. Abbott's son on the right. Bob's pram is on the extreme right.

Alexander William Sage, Coal Merchant who ran a coal delivery service from Berkswell Station Yard, seen here with his son Reg in the yard at Truggist Hill Farm, Truggist Lane.

Arthur Freeman and Arthur Thompson with Foal at Blind Hall Farm, 1920. Arthur's mother Mary Ann (Polly) Thompson was the tenant at Blind Hall at this time.

1910. Dick Thompson with Tedding Machine at Blind Hall, this was very dirty work, as the machine designed to turn Hay for drying, would fill your lungs with dust on a dry day, and cover you with water when the hay was wet.

Charles James Satchwell, Carriers of Barratt's Lane, provided a twice weekly service into Coventry, on Tuesday and Friday for 6d return, which included a charge for the Toll Man on Hearsall Common to open the toll gates. The picture is of passengers boarding the Cart outside Barnett Cottage, Back Lane, Four Oaks, in the late 1920's.

Poultry Plucking at Arnold Farm, this postcard which was posted on 23rd Jan 1909, was sent to Master D. Thompson, Four Oaks.

Frank Taylor whose son Wm. Docker Taylor sold the Butchers Shop to Sos Warmingham in the late 1930's, seen here with his delivery cart about 1910. At that time it will be seen that he was also Baking on the premises, the ovens are still retained at the back of the shop.

Frank and Sid Poole, Dairymen of Wootton Green Farm, Wootton Lane, delivering milk to property at the rear of the Railway Inn which is shown to the left of the drive.

A tranquil scene of Jimmy Underhill haymaking at Meadow Bank in the late 1940's with young Michael Hazeldine seen on the seat.

A photograph taken at Beechwood Farm with Bill Hurst on the tractor on the last occasion the corn was cut with a binder on which Phil Taylor is seen.

This photograph shows Rupert Arnold who was an agricultural contractor at the Haven, Four Oaks, where he is seen working at his saw bench being driven by a belt from his tractor. The wheel of his steam traction engine can just be seen parked at the side of Back Lane and on the opposite side of the lane the roof of Rock Farm. (Picture by permission of the Coventry Evening Telegraph).

Although a picture of Rupert Arnold's tractor could not be found in operation, this is a copy of the picture which hung in his home showing his tractor when first purchased from John Fowler & Company, Leeds.

Sos Warmingham taking delivery of the 'Best Beast' from Henley cattle Market, the driver of Eddie Hardy's cattle truck being Arthur Powell. The Manor House which was unfortunately demolished can be seen on the opposite side of the road to his shop.

Cecil (Sos) Warmingham's Butchers Shop, at 248 Station Road, was acquired from Wm. Docker Taylor whose family had established a Butchers Shop at these premises over 300 years before.

c 1932. (A. Mills, Cov). Henry Cox with his delivery bike outside his Newsagents and Stationary shop in Station Road, near the Railway Station. The newstand reporting 'Disaster Airship Sunk in North Sea, 16 drowned'.

Local Fed
Beef, Pork and Lamb

'Phone:
BERKSWELL 3132

C. WARMINGHAM
High-Class Family Butcher
STATION ROAD :: BALSALL COMMON

HOME MADE:
Sausage
Steak & Kidney Pies
Faggots

Killed on our
own Premises

Sos Warmingham as he will be remembered by everyone, inside his Shop at Station Road, which he ran for over fifty years.

This shop which was built on the corner of Windmill Lane by the owner in 1915, was a Grocers and Motor Spirit Service Station. This picture taken in the early 1920's shows Mr. Frederick H. Greenway whose shop was sold on his death in 1939. Also in the picture are his children Norah on the left, Joe on the right who himself died shortly afterwards and their friend Georgina Vincent in the middle.

This picture taken when the Village Forge was being rebuilt in 1968, shows estate workers, Stan Parr on the left, Ivor Mould and Burt Batchelor. Stan Parr was tragically killed at Blind Hall when he was knocked from the ladder on which he was working by a falling branch, when trees were being lopped.

SPECIAL OCCASIONS

A big event in the area early this century would have been the landing of this airship in a field near the "George in the Tree".

(M. Watson. Berk). This postcard issued in approximately 1909 shows a Bleriot monoplane sheeted over for the night being guarded, it is thought, by P.C. Ambrose Sommerton with a colleague and interested outlookers. In 1908 a prize of £10,000 was offered by Lord Northcliffe, owner of the Daily Mail to the first aviator who could travel between London and Manchester where his main offices were situated within 24 hours with a maximum of two stops for re-fuelling. Louis Paulham, a Frenchman, eventually winning the prize in 1910 covering the 185 miles in a Henry Farman in 4 hours 12 minutes at an average speed of 44 m.p.h.

May Day 1905. The procession emerging from the Rectory Gates, the school log book recording 'no school held', the girls met at the school at 8.30 am, formed a line and marched round the parish with their May Queen (Edith Timms) and Floral Wreaths. The Boys equivalence of this being November 5th when the Log book again records School closed. The boys according to custom perambulating the parish with an Efigy of Guy Fawkes. *(Frederic Lewis. Birm.).*

May Day 1906. The procession outside the school. The day looks cold but even so Mrs. Callow has put her caged bird over her doorway. The name of the May Queen was not recorded in the Log book this year, as the school was closed from March 16th until June 11th for alteration and repairs to be made to enlarge the school to accommodate 187 children. *(Frederic Lewis. Birm.).*

1910 Approx. The Coventry and Local sections of the "Manchester Unity Friendly Society Independent Order of Odd Fellows" shown outside the "Bear Inn". This was an annual procession which started from the Bear and was so important that the school closed to enable the junior members to take part. The Berkswell Loyal George Lodge group including Tom Batchelor and Mr. Hitchcock who kept the Village Shop are standing below the tree to the left of the picture.

(M. Watson, Berks) 1920. These local children were 'Kings Messengers' at a show put on at the Reading Room, to raise money for overseas Missions. Back row from left: Hilda Skidmore, Edie Powell, Jack Underhill, Nora Hiorns, Mabel Connell, John Kaye, Doug Smith, Kath Parker and Nellie Kaye. Middle row: Albert Rice, Marjorie Roake, Frank Potts, Jim Castle, Arthur Powell, Harold Harris, Harry Beecham, Phyllis Callow (now Mrs Edwards). Front row: Lionel Beecham, Betty Underhill, Anne Woolley, Rene Greasley, Ada Bassett, Sid Carter, Mabel Rice, Lilly Underhill.

1928. The funeral of Mrs. Christina Elizabeth Feeney, the wife of John Feeney whose father was the founder and owner of the Birmingham Post and Mail. As was the custom, the coffin was carried through the village, and is seen here headed by Mr Edward Pope (Bailiff), Mr. Geo. Powell, Gardener, and Mr. Harrison, Chauffeur. Mrs. Feeney who was a school manager, lived at The Moat, and is still remembered by local people for the good work that she did and especially the parties she gave to the school children.

The Berkswell and District, British Legion Brass Band leaving the Church after attending a service. They would then march to the Railway Station, where they would play outside the "Railway Inn" the quality of the playing apparently deteriorating quite fast due to the thirst the blowing created.

A picture taken inside the Bacon House at Home Farm in 1949 when a calf was presented to Miss Ann Wheatley by suppliers and Estate workers to mark the occasion of her forthcoming marriage. Those present from the left: Teddy Barr, Tom Whitehead, Betty Fisher, Bill Wilkinson, Alfie Carter, Sid Davis, Vic Bateman, Jack Mills, Gordon Barnett, Jim Squires, Lou Connelly and Miss Ann. *(Picture by permission of the Coventry Evening Telegraph)*.

This picture taken outside Berkswell Church porch in 1949 depicts the marriage of Ann, the daughter of Christobel and the late Charles Joshua Hirst Wheatley, to Captain Hubbard. After the ceremony the name Wheatley-Hubbard was adopted. *(Picture by permission of The Coventry Evening Telegraph)*.

This photograph taken on the occasion of Billy Tranter's retirement as Estate foreman, he being seen in the chair which was presented to him, in the middle of the group. Others present from left, standing: Charlie Leddington, Archie Cudmore, Albert Webb, Lou Connelly, with Bill Wilkinson (Arthur's dad) in front, Ted Treadwell, Jim Squires, Jack Woolley, Mrs. Christobel Wheatley, Ivor Mould, Vic Bateman, Harry Ford, Jack Mills, Ron Webber, Tracy Hodges and Jack Green. Seated: Harry Ayres, Gordon Barnett, and Bill McCartney.

This picture shows the procession and blessing of the plough outside the porch of Berkswell Church, this being a ceremony revived by the Rector of Berkswell the Rt. Rev. J.D. McKie who was at that time also the Assistant Bishop of Coventry. Also shown in the picture from the left: Capt. Wheatley-Hubbard and Mr. Charles Hope. Others in the group include Walter Thompson, Joe Grey, John Cotterill and, extreme right Bill Hurst.

The Birthday Party held in the Cafe to celebrate fifty years of the Berkswell Girls Club, at the event were, standing from left: Mrs. W. Sage, Florrie Thompson, Mrs. R. Sage, Mrs. Abbotts, Mrs. Turner, Mrs. Hartfield, Mrs. Worrod, Lilian Powell, Irene Fox (Nee Hurst), Nellie Harris, and Mrs. Poole. Sitting: Mary Thompson, Audrey Mears, May Goode, Mrs. Davies, Rose Thompson, Mrs. Connelly, Mrs. Christobel Wheatley and Mrs. Brett. *(Late 1950's)*

A presentation in the Cafe to two long service Bellringers, the Tankards being presented by the assistant Bishop of Coventry and the then Rector of Berkswell, Rt. Rev. J.D. McKie. The picture taken in the 1960's shows from the left: Arthur Powell, Eddie Hardy, Mr. Hope, Bishop McKie, Phillip Bonham, Harry Worrod, Ivor Nelson, Trevor Bonham, Mr. Whitehead and Patrick Hope.

BERKSWELL AT WAR

This postcard shows a group of Berkswell and Hampton Red Cross who were possibly V.A.D. nursing staff at the Rectory when a hospital during the 1914-18 War when this was issued. The view taken outside the Reading Room depicts Maud Watson in the dark uniform with Mrs. Harvey Smith on the right and Mrs. Moggs-Wright to the left of Maud Watson on the front row. Others in the group include Miss Gem, Lilian Sage (nee Hitchcocks), Mrs Simpson and Mrs. Reeves.

The Unveiling of the War Memorial by Lord Methuen in 1920. It was built of local sandstone to the design of Sir Charles Nicholson, on the site of the original church school. The memorial which was paid for by public subscription was consecrated by the Archdeacon of Warwick, the Ven. Hugh C.A. Back, the Rector of Berkswell at that time. *(M. Watson)*.

(M. Watson, Berk). Taken when Major General Sir H.B. Walker visited Berkswell in 1921 to review the Ex-Sevice Men of the Parish. Some of those shown in the group are Bill Underhill in the wheelchair, Fred Stockly and in the foreground to the right, Moggs Wright.

A view of the War Memorial in the 1930's on Remembrance Sunday showing 38 individual crosses placed in memory of the parishioners who lost their lives in the 1914-18 War.

A village scene in the 1920's thought to be a Remembrance Service as the crowd seem to be centred around the War Memorial.

This group taken in the Cafe gardens in 1943 is the local section of the Royal Observer Corps who had their post in Back Lane, Four Oaks. Those present include John Greenwood, middle front row with Alan James and Archie Cudmore to his right, Lou Connelly directly behind him, and Bert Vaughan and Wally Thompson to his left. Bert Wagstaff is also shown, extreme right middle row.

A photograph showing a group of volunteer workers taken around 1943. Front row from left: Mrs. Austin, Mrs. Walter Greasley, * , Maud Banks, Mabel Rowley, Mrs. Briscoe, Mrs. Smith, Miss Barber, Mrs. Jeffs, Mrs. Cleaver, Mrs. Jennings. Back row: Les Clarke, George Teague, Mrs. Ford, Bill Rowley, George Stephens, Mrs. Mary Laird, * , Mrs. Moggs-Wright and Roland Hitchcock.

A group of local A.F.S. (Auxiliary Fire Service) members taken with their appliances outside the George in the Tree during the Second World War. Those in the group with Charlie Nutt, shown in the middle of the front row, include Frank Lees, (Ken Lees' father), Frank Enstone, Eric Hollick, and Albert Kimberley, the son of the owner of Kimberley's garage.

This view shows the re-consecration of the War Memorial in 1950. The scene showing the Bishop of Coventry consecrating the additional inscriptions of ten parishioners who died in the 1939-45 Second World War. *(Picture by permission of The Coventry Evening Telegraph).*

PEACE, 1919,

PROGRAMME OF

PEACE CELEBRATIONS

TO BE HELD IN

BERKSWELL PARK,

(By kind permission of J. H. Wheatley, Esq.)

ON SATURDAY, JULY 19th, 1919.

5-0 p.m. ATHLETIC SPORTS.
Additional Amusements, Shooting, &c., going on all the time.
7-0 p.m. DANCING.

Athletic Sports.

CHILDREN.

Conducted by Messrs. J. FREWING and J. L. BRAIN.

	BOYS.	GIRLS.
4-0	1—100 Yards (Ages 8-10)	1—100 Yards (Ages 8-10)
	2—100 Yards (Ages 11-12)	2—100 Yards (Ages 11-12)
	3—100 Yards (Ages 13-15)	3—100 Yards (Ages 13-15)
	4—Sack Race (Open)	4—Catch-the-Train Race (Open)
	5—Potato Race (Ages 8-11)	5—Needle-threading Race (Ages 8-11)
	6—Potato Race (Ages 12-15)	6—Needle-threading Race (Ages 12-15)
	7—Three-legged Race (Open)	7—40 Yards (7 and under)

(Infants, Boys and Girls).

Prizes (for all the above)—First, 2/6 ; Second, 1/6 ; Third, 1/-

ADULTS.

Judges—J. H. WHEATLEY, ESQ., J.P. and CHARLES WHEATLEY, ESQ.
Starter—B. FRANCIS, ESQ.
Clerks of the Course—Messrs. P. BARFOOT, J. L. BRAIN and W. LONG.

		Prizes—First	Second	Third
5-0	1—50 Yards Sack Race ...	7 6	5 0	2 6
5-10	2—75 Yards Egg-and-Spoon Race for Women	7 6	5 0	2 6
5-20	3—Lightning-change Race for Ex-Service Men ...	£1	10 0	5 0
5-30	4—Threading-the-Needle Race for Women	7 6	5 0	2 6
5-40	5—100 Yards Three-legged Race ...	7 6	5 0	2 6
5-50	6—Blind-fold Potato Race for Women	7 6	5 0	2 6
6-0	7—100 Yards Flat Race for Ex-Service Men ...	£1	10 0	2 6
6-10	8—Obstacle Race ...	7 6	5 0	2 6
6-20	9—Tug-of-War for Men (in sets of 8) ...	Prize 16/-		
6-30	10—Tug-of-War for Women (in sets of 8) ...	Prize 16/-		
6-45	PRIZE DISTRIBUTION.	All Entries Free.		

Parishioners only will be allowed to compete in the above Events.
The Committee reserve to themselves the right to handicap at their discretion any candidate or candidates for Events, and to withdraw or alter any Race that may be deemed necessary on account of there not being sufficient entries or from any other cause.
The decision of Judges is final.

'Peace at Last'. Lets Celebrate.

All Parishioners who served in the First World War received one of these as a mark of respect from the people of Berkswell.

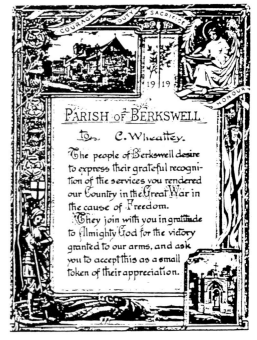

An extract from the Church School Log Book of November 1940.

15.11.40 Owing to a very severe air raid during the night 33 children were absent out of a total of 61 on the roll. Those present were extremely tired. The Correspondent came in and advised me to close at playtime in the afternoon session.

18.11.40 Since the air raid on Coventry on Friday night 50 odd people have had to be found sleeping quarters in the school

BERKSWELL AT PLAY

The Berkswell Band with their Conductor outside the "Railway Inn". Although the full names of the members are not known they do include Ted Walker, Billy Whitehead and Bill, Harry and Walter Greasley. The man on the extreme right is known to be Harry Taylor who was the Butcher in Berkswell Village, and was Peter Taylors' father.

The finish of a Motorcycle Trial outside the "George in the Tree" sometime in the 1930's. The gentleman standing to the right of the motorcycle and sidecar with the white scarf is thought to be the owner of Berkswell Hall, Colonel Charles Joshua Hirst Wheatley.

1910. The scene at the opening of the New Pavilion and Cricket Ground of the Berkswell Cricket Club at Green Lane, the ceremony being performed by Mrs. Feeney. The Club which was founded in 1897 had previously played on Berkswell Hill on the Coventry Road. Mr. Joshua Hirst Wheatley was the Club's first President.

The Berkswell Cricket Team at the time of the opening of the new Ground and Pavilion in 1910. Standing from left: Malcolm Watson, Oswald Jackson, W.B. Sage, W.A. Palmer, Dr. Smithies, R.C. Sage, John Smith (Umpire). Sitting: W.T. Greasley, F. Whinfrey, J.D. Stone (Capt), F. Cockersole, J. Edginton.

The Berkswell Cricket Club team by the mid 1930's had relegated Reg Sage to an Umpire as he is shown on the right. The other Umpire is Mervyn Hiorns and the gentleman on the left, Mr. W. Catterall, was some years earlier the Stationmaster at Berkswell Station.

The Berkswell Football Club team taken in 1931 at the ground on the Meriden Road. The team are back row from the left: Albert Chapman, Jack Underhill, Bill Cramner, Joe Wright, and Bill Squires. Front row: Ralph Howe, Bill Dyer, Les Dunne, Ron Dunne, Dick Nurser and Chuck Hazel.

Although not a sport, campanology plays an important part in village life. The size of the ringing area in the Church unfortunately did not permit all of the Bellringers to be recorded on this picture taken in the late 1960's. Len Skidmore is on the left, Arthur Powell in the middle and a young Robin Hope now the Captain of the Bellringers on the right.

PROGRAMME

in connection with the celebration of

HIS MAJESTY'S CORONATION

On WEDNESDAY, MAY 12th, 1937,

to be held in

BERKSWELL PARK.

(By kind permission of Col. C. J. H. Wheatley)

2·30 Service in Berkswell Church.

3·15 Children's Athletic Sports.

4·30 Children's Tea and Distribution of Prizes for Children's Sports in Stable Yard.

4·30 Adults' Athletic Sports.

5·15 Maypole Dance by Children.

5·30 Adults' Tea in Stable Yard.   1st Sitting.

6·45 Ditto   ditto   2nd Sitting.

7·30 Distribution of Prizes for Adult Sports at the winning post by Sir Charles Hyde, Bart.

8·0   Dancing on the Lawn (weather permitting).

10·0 Bonfire and Fireworks. (People are requested to keep the Hall side of the lake).

E. J. Kennard, Printer, Warwick St., Leamington Spa.

Athletic Sports

Judges:
SIR CHARLES HYDE, Bart., MAJOR HUGGINS, Messrs. T. BARNACLE, H. SMITH, E. HARDY.
Starter: Mr. H. TAYLOR.   *Clerk of the Course:* Mr. SIMPSON.
Children's Sports: Miss TATERSALL, Mrs. SMITH.

1st, 2nd, 3rd and 4th Prizes in each event.

1	Boys, 5—6, 40 yards Flat Race	7	Boys, 11—13, 100 yards Flat Race
2	Girls, 5—6, 30 yards Flat Race	8	Girls, 11—13, 50 yds. Three-legged Race
3	Boys, 11—13, 100 yds. Obstacle Race		
4	Girls, 11—13, 80 yards Flat Race	9	Boys, 7—10, 80 yards Flat Race
5	Boys, 7—10, 80 yards Obstacle Race	10	Girls, 7—10, 30 yds. Three-legged Race
6	Girls, 7—10, 50 yards Flat Race		

ADULT SPORTS.

		1st	2nd	3rd
1	75 yards Flat Race for unmarried women ...	10/-	6/-	2/6
2	120 yards Hurdle Race (open)	10/-	6/-	2/6
3	50 yards Egg and Spoon Race for women	7/6	5/-	2/6
4	100 yards Three-legged Race (women and men paired) ...	15/-	10/-	5/-
5	50 yards Flat Race for married women	10/-	6/-	2/6
6	440 yards Obstacle Race	10/-	6/-	3/-
7	200 yards Flat Race for men under 30	10/-	6/-	2/6
8	Threading Needle Race	7/6	5/-	2/6
9	50 yards Sack Race (open)	10/-	6/-	2/6
10	80 yards Veterans' Handicap (yard for years over 30 to 60)	10/-	6/-	2/6
11	150 yards Handicap for *bona fide* farm labourers ...	10/-	6/-	2/6
12	Tug-of-War for men, in sets of eight	20/-	12/-	

All entries free.

Parishioners only will be allowed to compete in any of the above events.

Not more than two first prizes or three in all will be awarded to any competitor.

The Committee reserve the right to refuse any entry, also to handicap at their discretion any candidate or candidates for all events and to alter any race that may be deemed necessary.

The decision of Judges is final.

OTHER COMPETITIONS.

Bowling for Pig
Pig given by Col. Wheatley
Charge, 3 balls for 3d.

......

Striking for a Leg of Mutton
Leg of Mutton given by Mr. H. Taylor
Charge, 1d. a try

......

Walking Millionaire
Charge, 2 balls for 1d.

This programme in connection with the celebration of His Majesty King George VI Coronation, is typical of the many events held in Berkswell Park over the years.

This aerial view of Berkswell Hall taken on the occasion of the last Church Fete to be held at the Hall in 1984 prior to the Hall being sold and turned into flats. This photograph was taken by Phil Harvey from one of the microlight aircraft which proved such a success at this event.

Another view taken on the same occasion showing St. John Baptist Church and also the Old Rectory, now the Well House. The tennis courts where Maud Watson and her sister Lilian learned to play, and the flower beds still visible in the lawn can be seen.

c 1908. (Frederic Lewis. Birm.). The 'South' Lodge of The Moat Estate of John Feeney which was built in 1892 to give Mr. Feeney a quicker route to Berkswell Railway Station via Baulk Lane.

This postcard, issued in the early 1930's shows Yew Tree Farm on the corner of Spencer's Lane and Baulk Lane, at the time it was occupied by Frank Hiorns and his family.

c. 1920 (M. Watson, Berk.). This postcard shows Lavender Hall, when it was farmed by Thomas Malcolm Smith. The view shows the front of this 16th century dwelling which was re-faced in brick at a later date, and the barn can be seen on the left.

c. 1936 (Thompson, Cov.). This postcard shows Berkswell Lane, now Lavender Hall Lane, looking towards the village with Lavender Hall barn on the right and Fernbank opposite.

Mercote Hall which was the original 'Dower House' of Berkswell Estate is seen here in it's glory prior to becoming in the 1914/18 War, a Camp for German Prisoners. Due to the damage which was caused to the property, it was never lived in again, fell into disrepair and was finally demolished in 1936.

Tom Batchelor Senior who was Head Gardener at Mercote Hall seen here working in one of the greenhouses. When members of the Mitchell family were in residence he would take them on Sunday mornings, boating on Mercote Mill Pool, which at that time was large enough to sail on.

Mercote Hall 1913. At that time it was rented as a weekend retreat by the Birmingham "Mitchell" Brewery family. All that now remains of the property is the Barn seen on the right which is used for the storage of agricultural machinery.

Tom Batchelor Junior with younger sister May, later to become May Goode seen here with their bicycles on one of the pathways of Mercote Hall gardens. Cycling on these paths was a pleasure only possible when the Mitchell family were not in residence.

c 1905. (Frederic Lewis. Birm). Ram Hall shown on this postcard is a fine early Tudor building with stone mullion windows. The Hall is part of the Berkswell estate, the tenant farmer at the time being Thomas Fletcher.

c 1906. (Frederic Lewis. Birm.). Blind Hall Farm which is part of the Berkswell Estate, was Tenant farmed at this time by William Brown and his sister Sarah. Blind Hall Lane on which the hall is situated was the original coaching road to Coventry, to save the climb up Berkswell Hill.

c 1905. (Frederic Lewis. Birm.). Hill House, Coventry Road. Part of the Berkswell Estate, the tenant at the time of this postcard being Thomas Clements. After his death, in 1923 the house was occupied by Charles Wheatley and his new bride Christobel, and they remained there until the death of Mr. Wheatley's father when they then moved to Berkswell Hall.

c 1906. (Frederic Lewis. Birm). Mount Pleasant, Truggist Lane. This fine residence was at that time still a part of the Berkswell Estate, and the tenant was Mr. Petigrue and family.

The house on the corner of Meriden Road and Back Lane shown on this postcard in 1904, has the owner known as old man Ridley standing by the fence. The weathervane is unusual turning and at the same time registering on a dial. When the horse was eventually removed it was found to be full of holes, as the local sharpshooters had been using it for target practice.

c 1908. (Frederic Lewis. Birm.). The Four Oaks crossroads where the Meriden and Hampton Turnpike roads met. The four Oaks planted in 1800 can be seen, the one on the far left already dead and was eventually felled. The cameraman's motorcycle and sidecar is again in the picture.

c 1914. (C.W. Selby, Birm). The Meet either assembling or having just lost the scent of the Fox at Four Oaks.

c. 1917 (W. Holmes. Birm.). This view of Waste Lane is taken just after the intersection with Windmill Lane looking towards Coventry with Meadow Farm on the left.

This postcard, issued by Russell of Balsall, which shows Tower House, called by locals Cow Pen Castle was posted in 1911 when the house would have been occupied by R.E.S. Wyatt and his parents. Bob Wyatt went on to become captain of Warwickshire Cricket Club and later of England, being capped forty times. On the left of the picture can be seen Home Farm, now called Canterbury House.

c 1908. (Frederic Lewis. Birm.). This postcard shows Carol Green junction with Truggist Lane bearing to the left, and Tower House on the corner. On the road to Berkswell through the trees can be seen Fir Tree Cottage and The Croft and also the photographer's motorcycle.

THE WINDMILL BERKSWELL.

This postcard posted in Balsall Common in 1915, shows the Windmill and cottage owned at that time by John Hammond. The Windmill on the site of an earlier Post Mill was built in 1826. It was driven by sail until 1933 and then by diesel engine until 1948. It has since been fully restored.

MAGPIE HALL BERKSWELL

c 1918. (A. Mills. Cov.). This postcard of Magpie Hall in Magpie Lane shows a view of this 16th century farmhouse which has remained virtually unaltered to this day, with the exception of now having a television aerial on the roof.

This postcard of about 1906 gives us a view of the platform for Coventry with possibly the Stationmaster of the day Joseph Leveson Simpson waiting to ensure that the milk churns are loaded on the the next train. The line to Kenilworth is seen curving away to the right.

c 1913. (Frederic Lewis. Birm.). This view taken from the Coventry platform looking across the line to the booking office and Birmingham platform on the other side of the crossing gates.

The date of this postcard is 1932 by which time the footbridge had been built over the track and the two platforms are now opposite to each other on the Birmingham side of the crossing gates. The signal box can be seen on the right-hand side of the track on the opposite side of the level crossing.

This postcard of the late 1930's shows a three cylinder compound steam locomotive No. 1153 emerging from BeachwoodTunnel en route to Coventry. The message on the rear of the postcard reading 'Engine driver misjudged the time he had to relieve himself'.

A view showing the Railway Inn in the 1930's, with the entrance of the railway station and crossing gates shown in the background. The Publican at that time would have been William Henry Tongue.

A view from Truggist Lane looking at the level crossing gates with the Railway Inn in the background. The hoardings advertising among other items, Betta biscuits at 6d a packet would put the date at about 1936, the boys would be collecting train numbers, this LMS line at that time having 'Royal Scots' and 'Jubilees' steaming through at regular intervals.

Coventry Cycling Clubs' Alliance.   Berkswell, Sunday, May 31st, 1908.

The caption of this postcard tells the occasion but does not record how the publican of the 'Brickmakers Arms' behind which this field is situated would have satisfied the demands of so many customers. The view is taken looking towards the station. *(Jackson & Son, Cov.).*

c 1928. A view taken from outside the Brickmakers' Arms, looking down Station Road with the Railway Station in the background. The coal cart seen outside possibly belonging to William Sage who operated at that time from the Station Yard. He could well be having his 'Lunch' with the Publican Alfred Hainsworth.

c 1938. (Thompson. Cov.). The Brickmakers' Arms, Station Road. The customers inside could possibly be charged later, by the local policeman P.C. Thornborough of being drunk in charge of their bicycles.

c 1906. (Frederic Lewis. Birm.). This postcard of the George in the Tree at the time when the publican would have been Frederick Mundy, shows one of the staff preparing to use the heavy roller on the Croquet lawn at the rear. The width of the main Kenilworth — Stonebridge Road is worthy of note.

THE GEORGE-IN-THE-TREE HOTEL, TEL. 18 BERKSWELL

THE MOTORISTS RENDEZVOUS

CATERING & ACCOMMODATION

BERKSWELL. WARWICKSHIRE

This advertising postcard issued in the early 1920's shows an array of early road transport and indicates that the hotel is a rendezvous for motorists and was residential at that time. The telephone number for bookings is Berkswell 18.

TENNIS AND CROQUET LAWN, "GEORGE-IN-THE-TREE," BERKSWELL. SIDWELL, MERIDEN

c 1906. (Sidwell, Meriden). This postcard shows the Tennis & Croquet lawn at the rear of the George in the Tree with participants and spectators preparing for a game. This area is now completely covered by the car park.

LOCAL VILLAGES

BALSALL COMMON

This postcard issued in the early 1920's shows the Station Road — Kenilworth Road crossroads before the island was there with Gill Hollick's chemist's shop and Regent House on the corner, these premises now being occupied by Warwick Estates.

c 1929 (Thompson, Cov). This postcard shows the Kenilworth Road — Station Road junction with Regent House in the centre and Kimberley's garage on the left.

A photograph showing Kimberley's garage in the mid 1930's with Mr. & Mrs. Kimberley and their son beside the petrol pumps. The signs are interesting, one stating 'Fill up here with Shell', the other board being held by a Michelin Man advising customers 'No Russian sold here' a dig at R.O.P. petrol which was available at that time.

c 1908. (Frederic Lewis. Birm.) A beautiful rural scene taken at Grange Farm showing possibly the daughter of Elias Maisey who farmed the Grange at that time. The Hay Waggon completes the scene.

Although indicating Berkswell this postcard of 1910 shows a group of children outside The Little School, which used to be at the top of Holly Lane, where the Scout and Guide Headquarters now stands.

The Cinema which is shown here in the 1960's with the children it is assumed about to enjoy a special performance, was originally called The Berkswell Picture House, becoming the Cameo in later years.

c. 1932. (Thompson, Cov.). This delightful postcard of the Saracen's Head taken when the publican was Mrs. Helen Edith Mercedes Griffiths, shows a group of locals gathered for a Sunday morning drink.

"THE WHITE HORSE INN," BERKSWELL.   SIDWELL, MERIDEN.

c 1908. (Sidwell, Meriden). The 'White Horse Inn' with the narrow road stretching towards Kenilworth on the right. The Publican of the day Mrs. Selina Thomas and her family standing in the doorway.

c. 1921. (A. Mills. Cov.). Although this postcard indicates Station Road, Berkswell it is a view in Balsall looking down Station Road towards the station with Munton's Stores on the right. The small cottage in the distance on the left is where Dr. English had his surgery.

MUNTON'S STORES,
Station Road, BALSALL,
PROVISION SPECIALIST.

FAMILY GROCER.   TEA DEALER.   MERCHANT.
BOOT & SHOE FACTOR, & GENERAL STORES.
All Goods obtainable here are of FIRST quality.

Phone : BERKSWELL 60.

C. CHATTAWAY
& SONS

STATION ROAD
BALSALL COMMON
near Coventry.

OIL AND GENERAL HARDWARE DEALERS

Our Vans serve all Local Districts Weekly.

This picture taken in the late 1930's outside No. 213 Station Road shows Doris Lees, nee Chattaway, with young Ken in her arms. Ken's mother and father lived above the shop when they were first married. This shop has changed very little except the stock today does not include so many paraffin lamps.

Miss Warner standing outside her Grocers Shop in Station Road, this Store was originally "Munton's" and is shown opposite. The shop to the left was that of the Stationer and Printer, David Gee.

This shot of Frank Enston standing outside the door of his shop which is next door to that of Charlie Chattaway's shown on the opposite page, was most likely taken on the same day. Frank, who charged the local children 3d to cut their hair, seems to have a good supply of Brylcreem in his window.

MERIDEN

Cyclist's Memorial Meriden (The Unveiling)

(Sidwell, Meriden). This postcard was issued in 1921 and shows Lord Birkenhead carrying out the unveiling of the Cyclist's Memorial which was erected 'To the lasting memory of those Cyclists who died in the Great War 1914 – 19'.

c 1909. (Frederic Lewis. Birm.). This view of Main Road, which was the Birmingham Road, shows two groups of cottages with the Old Cross in it's original position on the Green opposite. The lady standing at the door of the first cottage (Darlaston Cottage) is advertising 'Teas provided' and the delivery cart is outside the newsagents and general store which was at that time Warmingham's.

THE BULL'S HEAD HOTEL, MERIDEN.   SIDWELL, MERIDEN

c 1907. (Sidwell, Meriden). The 'Bulls Head' Hotel, described at the time as offering every accommodation for travellers and cyclists, good stabling and posting. The Arch into the stable yard is seen on the left. The Publican at the time was Mrs. Elizabeth Boden.

A Postcard showing the Cyclist's Memorial Service being held some time in the mid 1930's.

The 'Queens Head' Meriden, would have been managed by Arthur Stoney in 1932, at the time of issue of this postcard. The Inn has remained generally unaltered with the exception of the Pump and buckets where the main entrance now is and a single pony and trap tethered where a row of cars are now a more normal sight.

BURTON GREEN

c 1910 (A.G. Studios. Cov.). The 'Peeping Tom' Inn on Cromwell Lane, when the publican, who can be seen at the doorway was Mr. Edward Cox.

TILE HILL

This postcard of Tile Hill shows the crossroads at Banner Lane looking towards Station Avenue. The card issued in the late 1920's shows the Shop and Cafe on the left and the 'Bell Inn' is in the opening on the right by the horse and cart.

THE "BELL" INN, TILE HILL   SIDWELL, MERIDEN.

c 1907. (Sidwell, Meriden). The 'Bell Inn' shown here with a very narrow Station Ave. to the left. As this postcard would be taken at the wish of the publican, the lady holding the baby would be Mrs. Emma Molesworth, the publican at the time.

A postcard issued in the late 1920's showing Tile Hill Station from Cromwell Lane looking towards Tile Hill Village. The signal box is seen in it's original position on the left on the same side as the Birmingham Platform, with the ticket office and Coventry Platform shown on the right.

The view on this postcard of the 1920's shows George Duggins, the father of the present George Duggins outside his blacksmith's shop on Duggins Lane. We are looking towards Tile Hill village with Conway Avenue, which was unadopted at the time, being on the left by the lamp post.

BARSTON

c 1906. (Frederic Lewis. Birm.). This postcard posted to Miss. F. Fletcher, Rock Farm, Back Lane, shows the 'Bulls Head' Barston. The publican at the time was Harry Williams, who it will be seen caters for Dinner and Tea parties.

MEER END

Although this late 1920's postcard says Berkswell, the 'Plough Inn' is of course at Meer End. The publican at the time was Ben. T. Williams, the brother of Mr. Harry Williams who with Jack Judge composed 'Its a long long way to Tipperary' in the 1914/18 War. Ben Williams is seen here with his wife outside the pub now known as the 'Tipperary Inn'.

STONEBRIDGE

The 'Stonebridge Hotel' as it looked in the late 1880's when it was a Coaching Inn. At that time it was managed by the Hartill Brothers.

c 1936. (Thompson. Cov.). The Stonebridge Hotel seen here with the original Coaching Inn incorporated into it, in the centre of the picture. The Hotel was residential and by the number of large saloons outside it appears that the picture was taken on a busy weekend.

The Ball Room, Stonebridge Hotel

c 1936 (Thompson, Cov.). This postcard produced for Alfred C. Crombleholme, who was the publican at the time shows the Ball Room at the Stonbridge Hotel. The splendour of this room and the Hotel in general, makes it seem a tragedy that the hotel had to be demolished.

A group of early motorists arriving at the Stonebridge Hotel sometime in the early 1920's, as carbide lamps are still fitted to the motorycle. Although the driver of the car seems to be in control, it is obvious who is issuing the instructions.

HAMPTON IN ARDEN

c 1908 (Frederic Lewis. Birm.) This early postcard showing the Post Office, is interesting in that it shows a notice requesting recruits for His Majesty's Army. Also, over the doorway are advertisements for Sydney Bradley Marriott, Painter and Decorator and J.J. Fitter, Watch & Clockmaker. The Post Office is also a collecting point for the Perth Dye works.

This postcard posted in 1905, shows the White Lion public house at a time when Mrs. Lucy Sames was the publican. On the opposite side of the road are the Church gates with a carriage and grey awaiting someone possibly at morning service.

DORRIDGE

This postcard posted in 1916, showing a badly surfaced Poplar Road, with a coal cart standing opposite Frank Aldington's shop the awning of which informs that he is a Fruiterer, Fish, Rabbit and Poultry Salesman. The shop next door is that of Henry Charles Wilson, Bicycle dealer.

KNOWLE

Dated 1926 this postcard shows the 'White Swan' Inn, High Street, and also the 'Red Lion' further down the street with an open topped, solid tyred Midland Red Bus parked outside.

ACKNOWLEDGEMENTS

Ted & Phyllis Edwards
Jane Edwards (nee Lees)
Bob Fletcher
Mrs. A.M. Fryer
May Goode
Nellie Harris (nee Kaye)
May Hardy
Phil Harvey
Mrs. C. Jagger
Arthur James
Millicent Kaye
Theresa Kendrick
Richard Lawton
Arthur & Lilian Powell
Elsie Powell
Mr. R.H. Pratt
Clem Satchwell
Len Skidmore
Bob & Margeret Thompson
Bert Wagstaff
Arthur & Joan Walker
Sos Warmingham
Mrs. Ernie Webb
Ron & Dolly Webber
Arthur Wilkinson
Mrs. E. Williams
Charles & Olive Woolley
Anne, Jack & Ken Woolley
Josie Yates
Mrs. D. Young

Due to the large number of people who helped with material for this book, the compiler would like to apologise if anyone has been omitted from this list.